MW00899975

CONTENTS

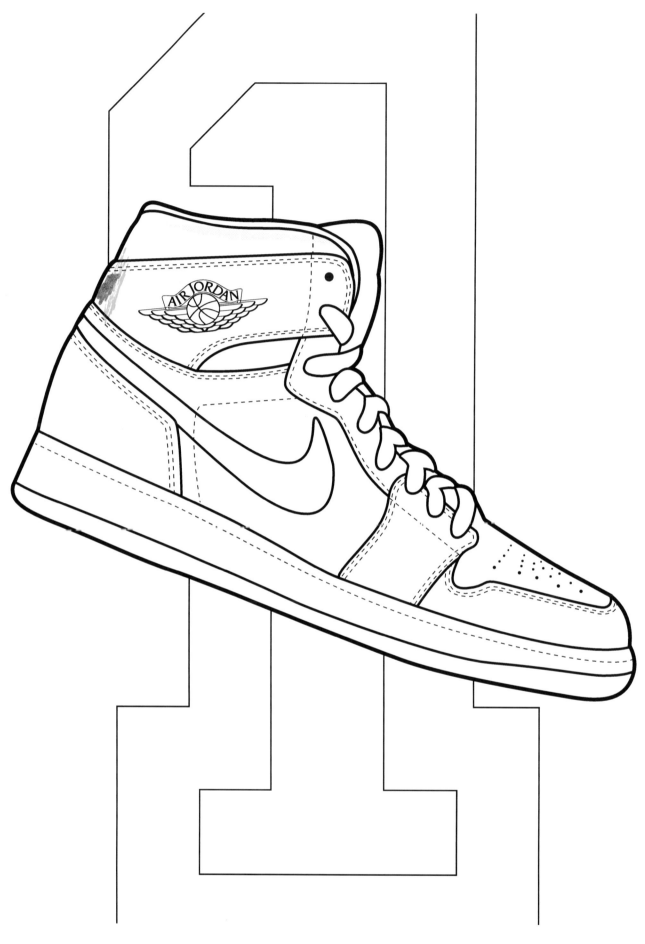

1

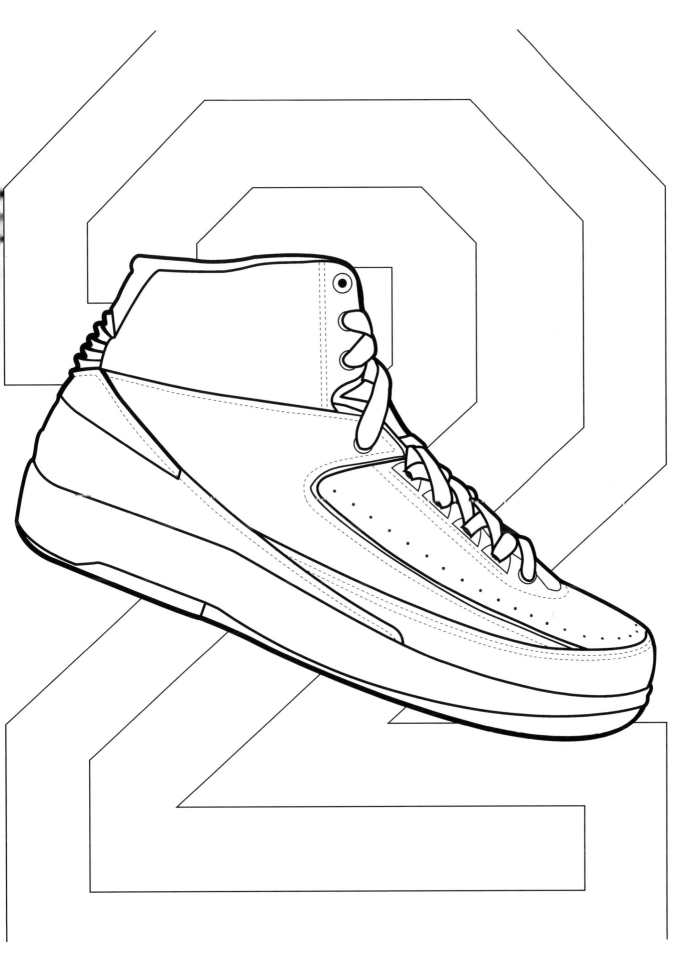

GK™

2

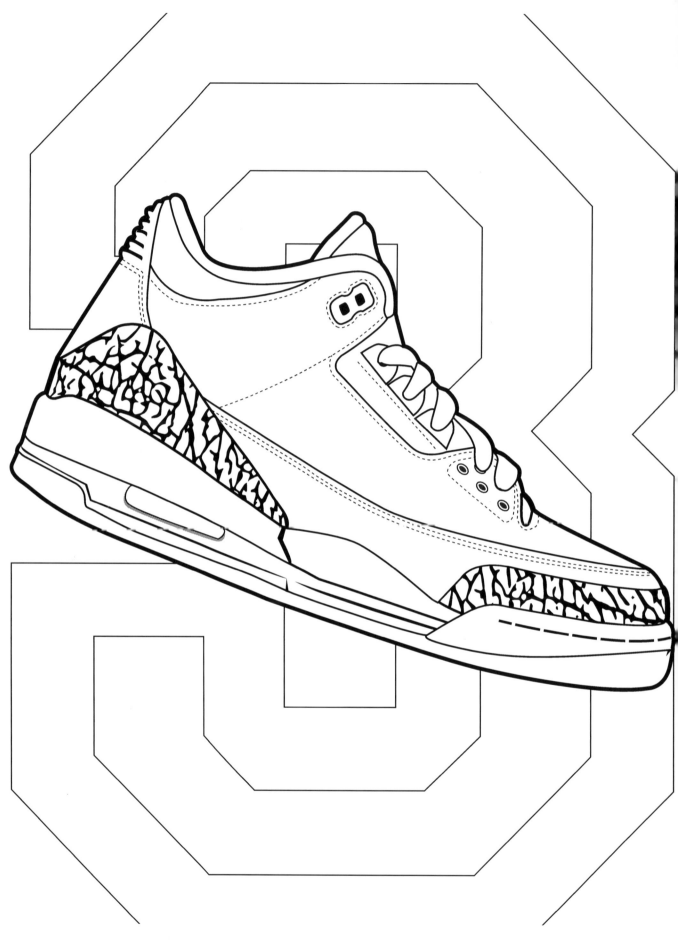

3

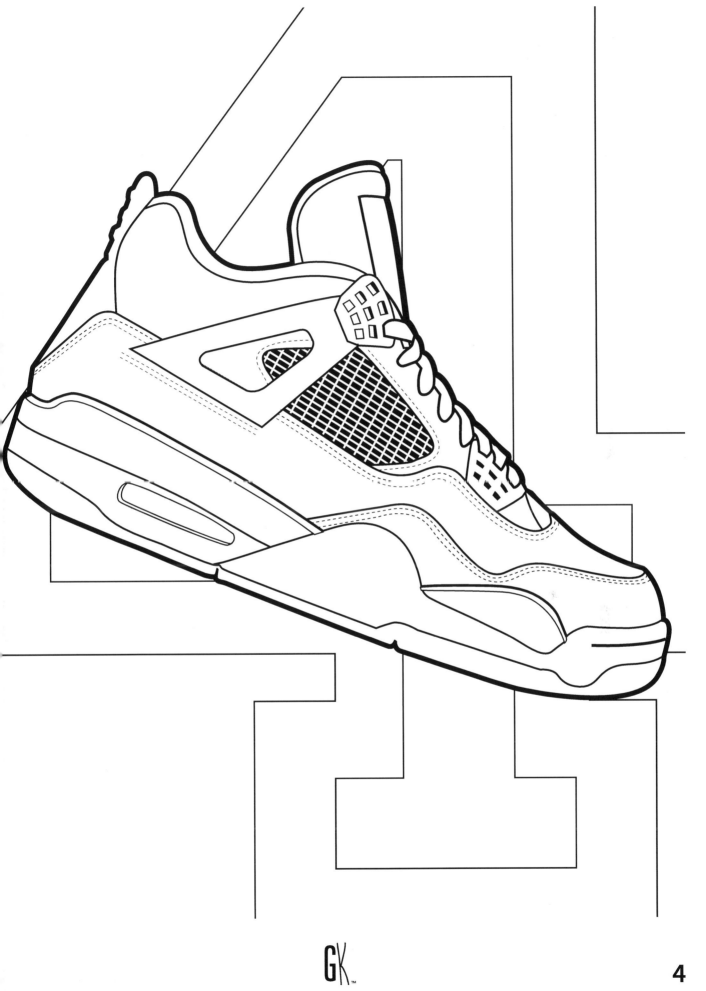

GK

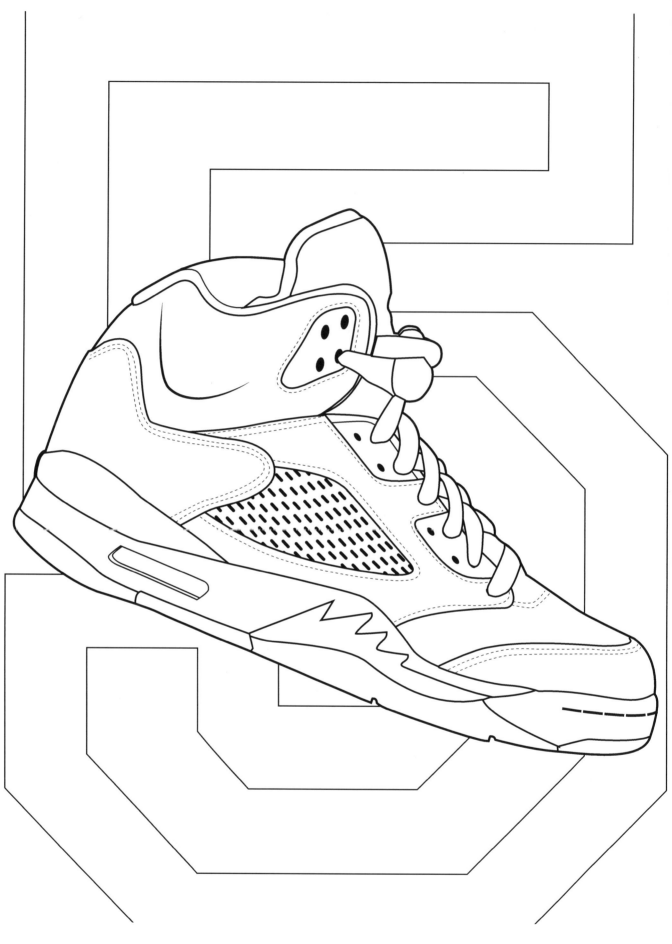

GK™

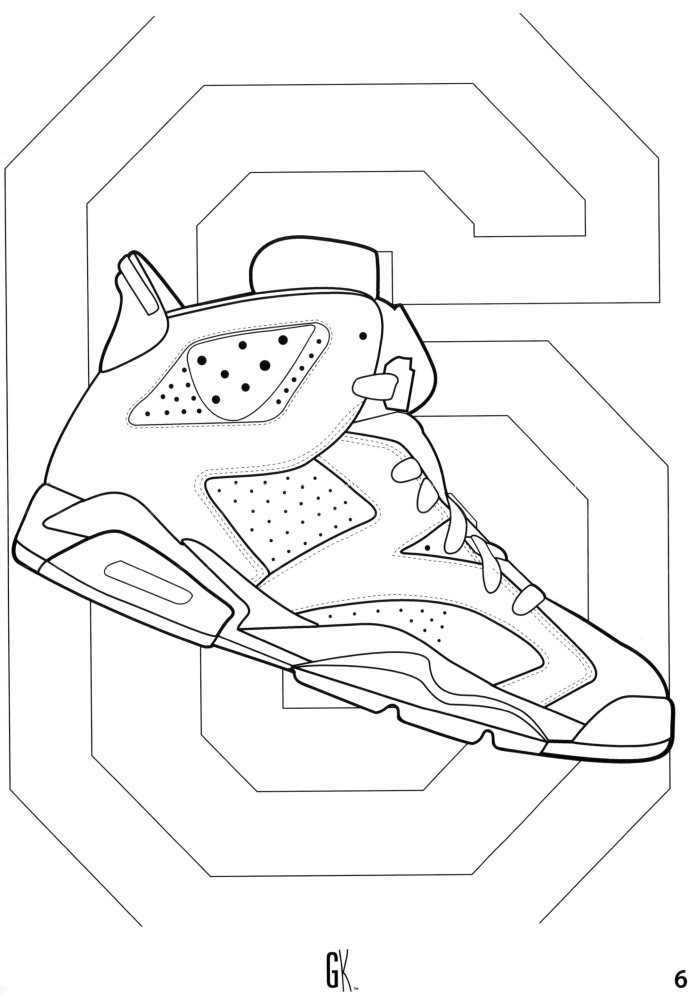

GK™

6

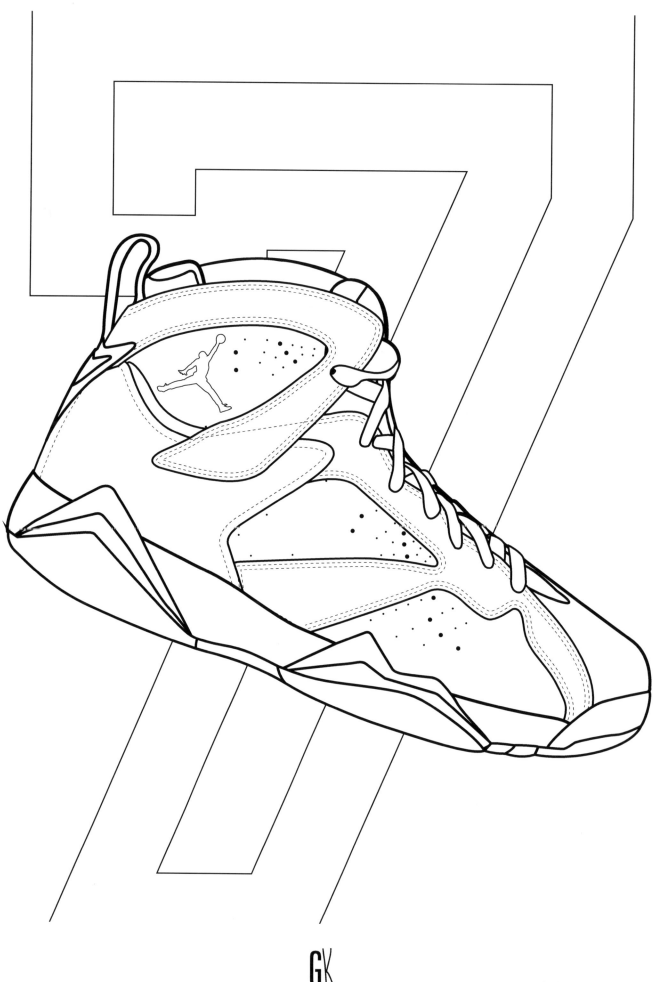

GK™

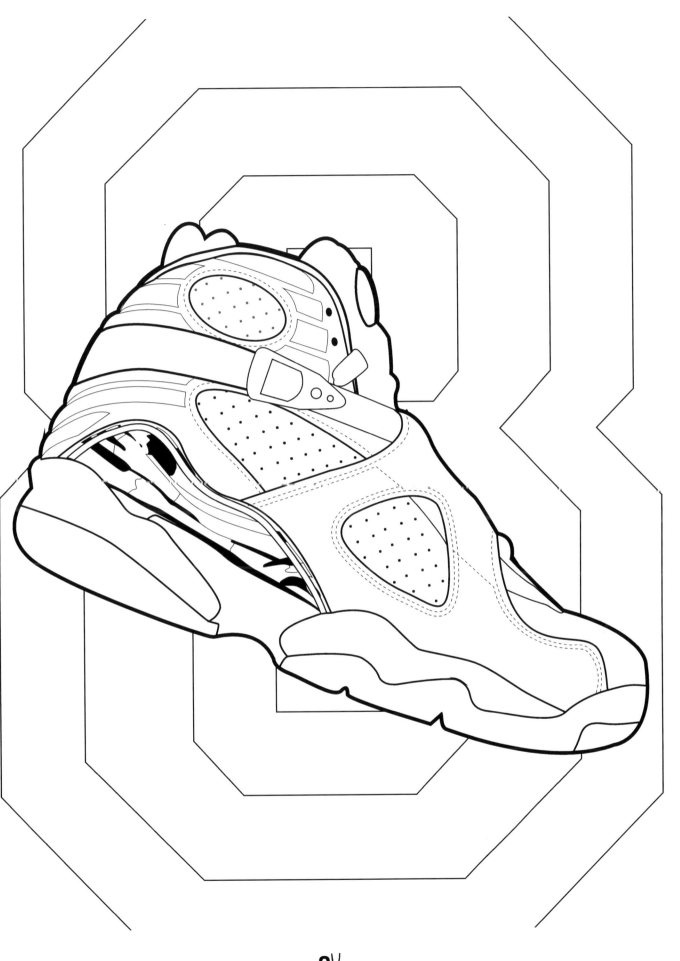

GK™

8

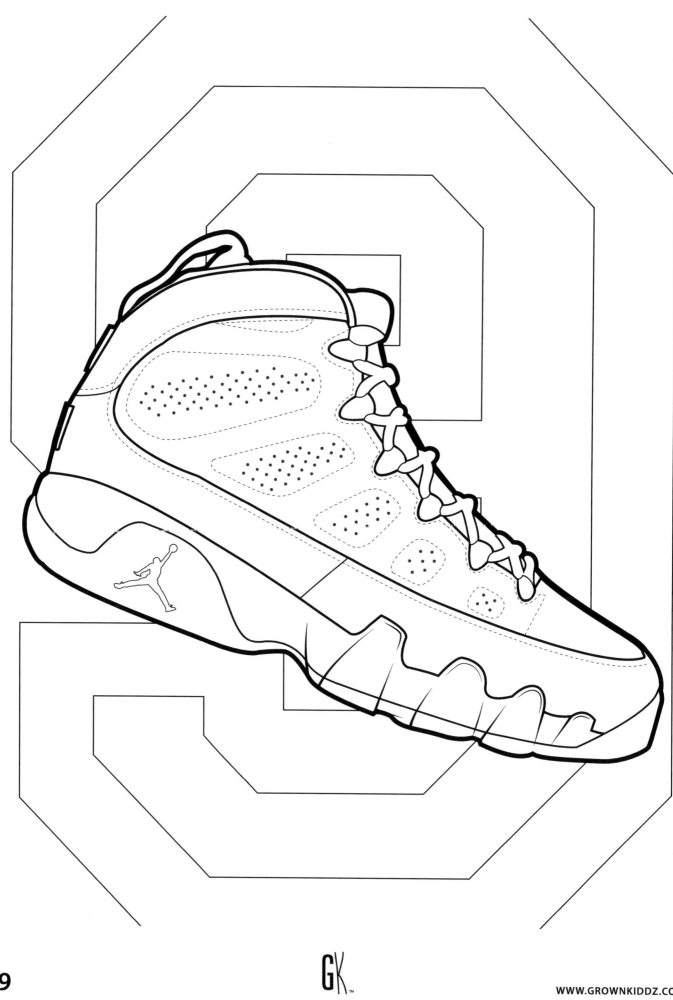

9

GK™

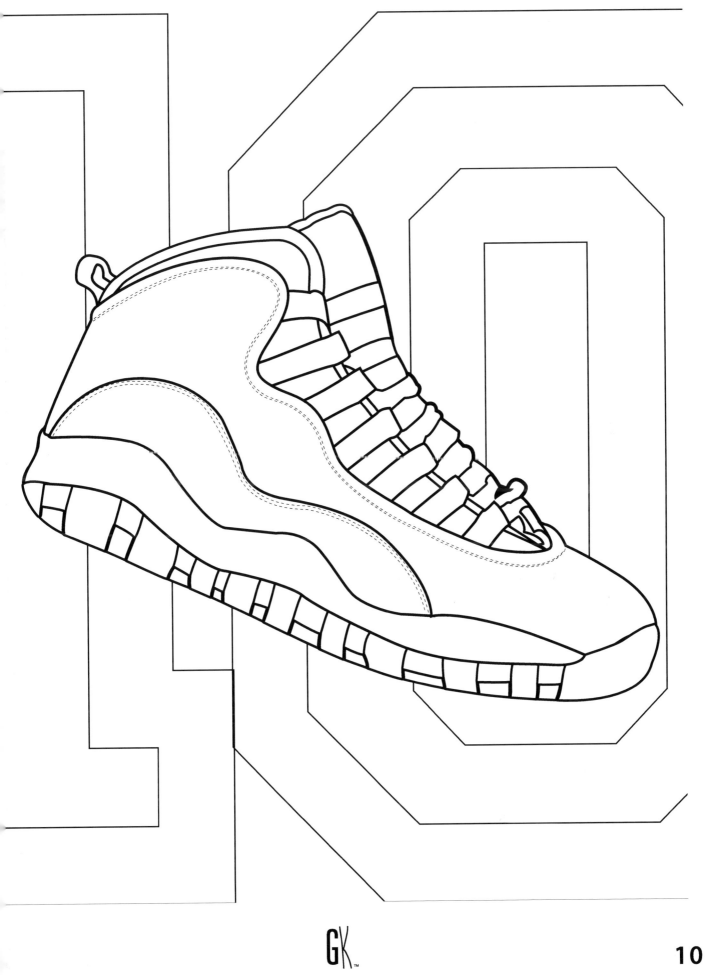

GK™

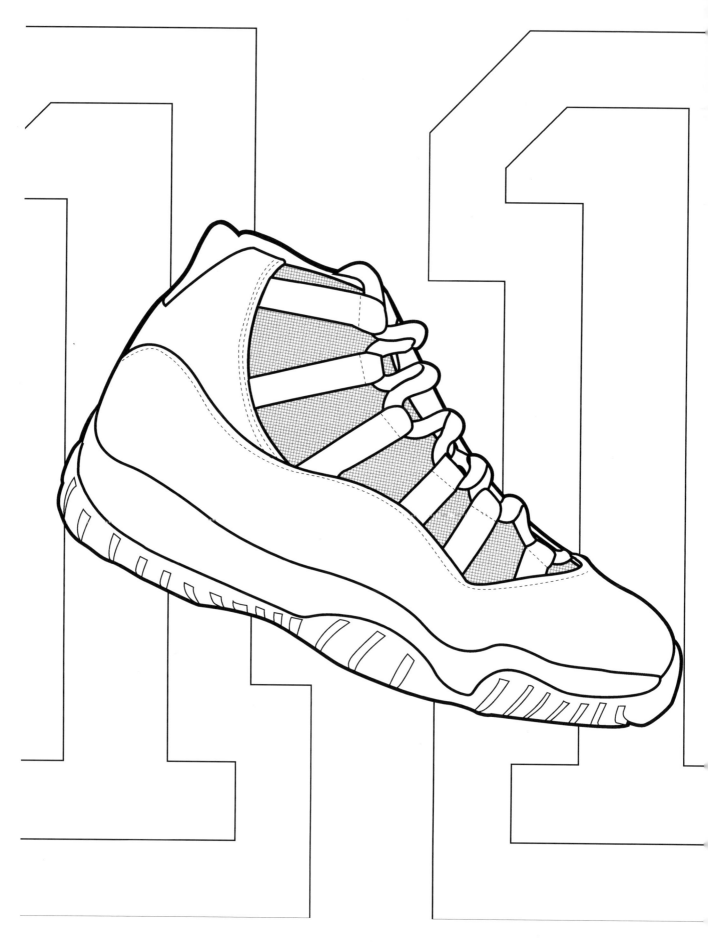

11

GK™

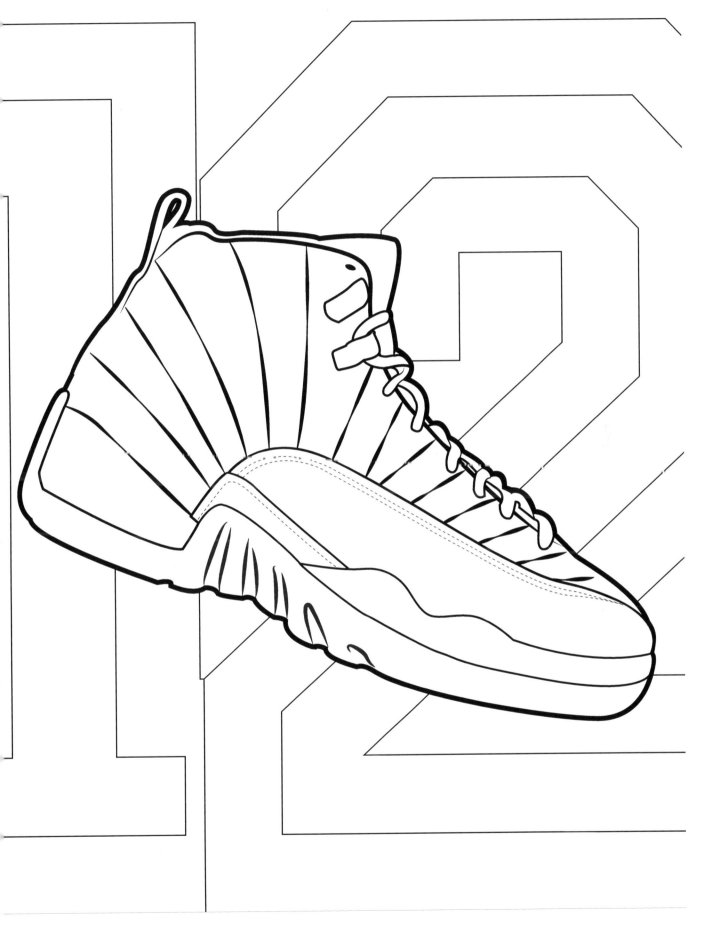

GK™

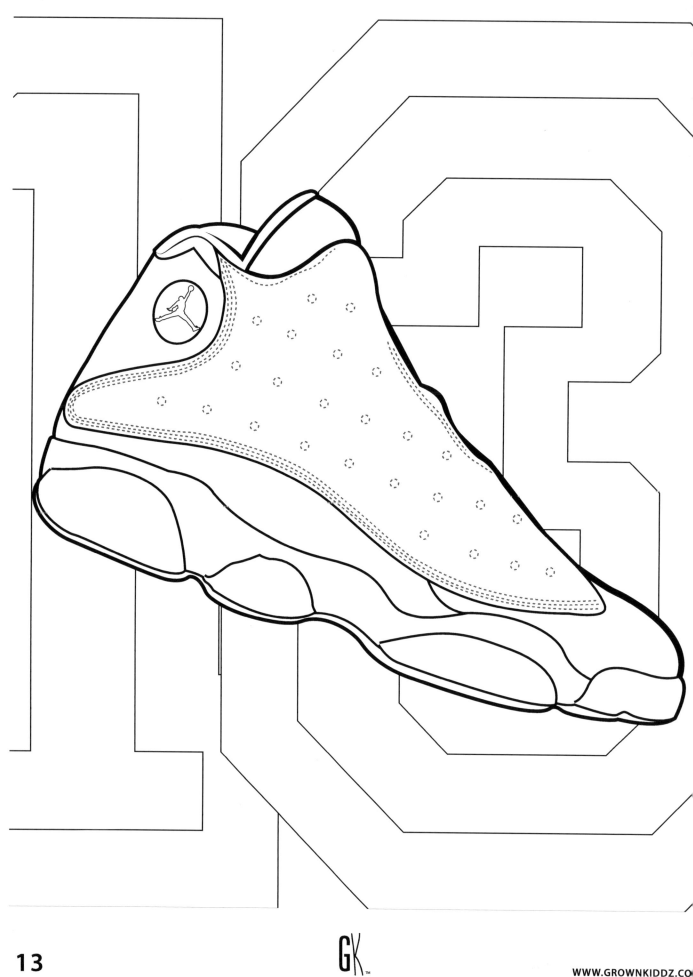

13

GK™

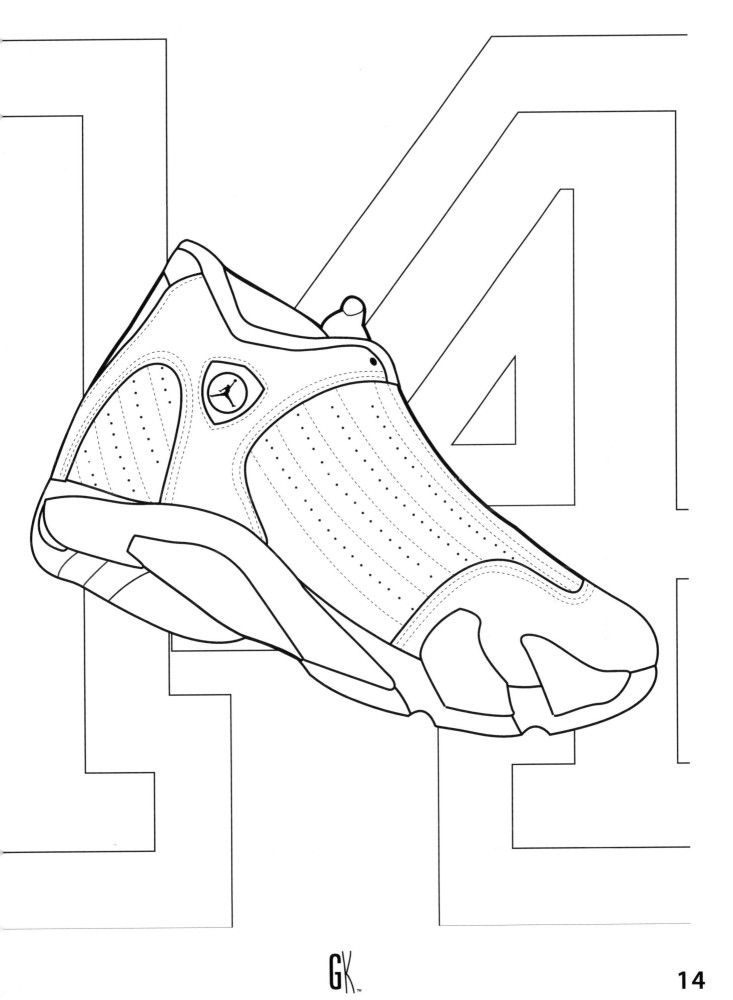

GK

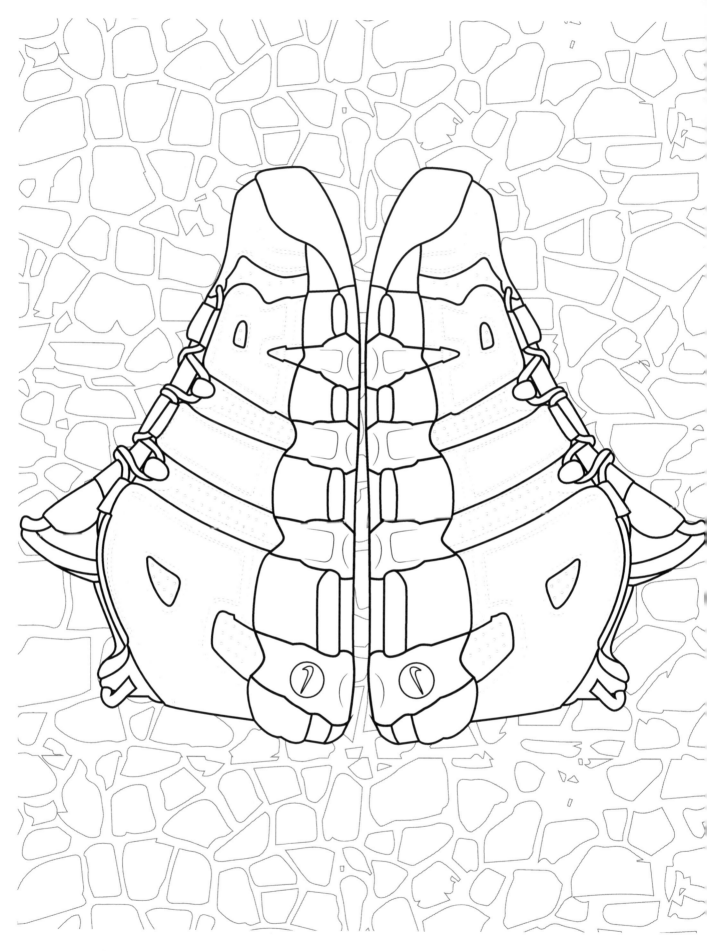

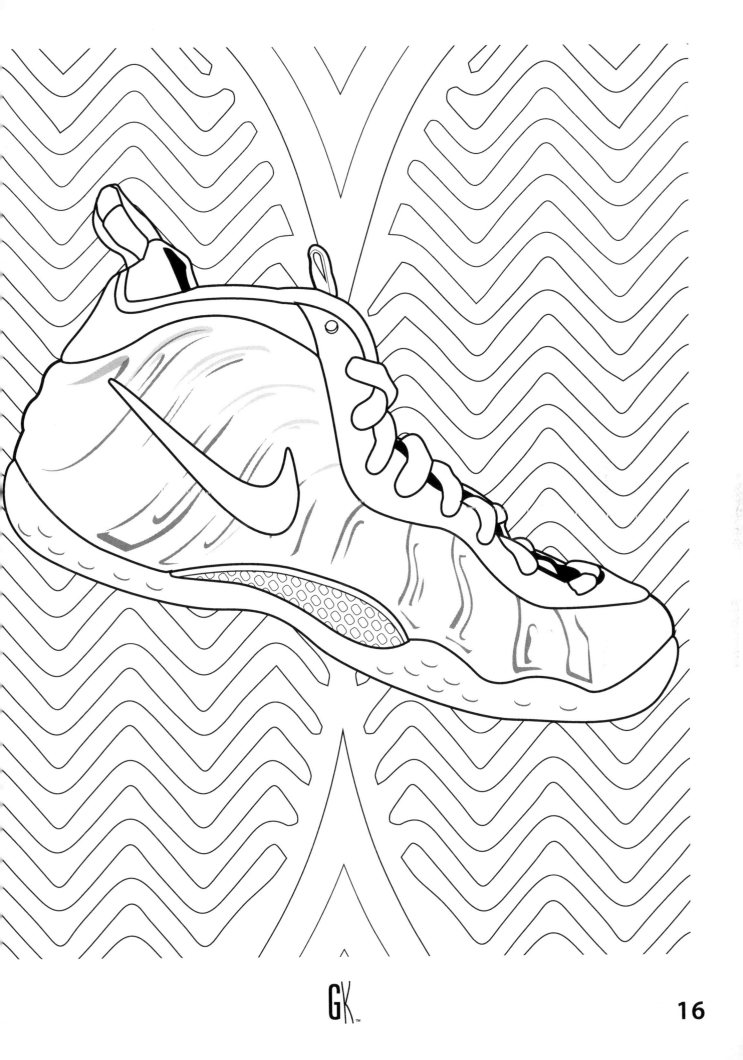

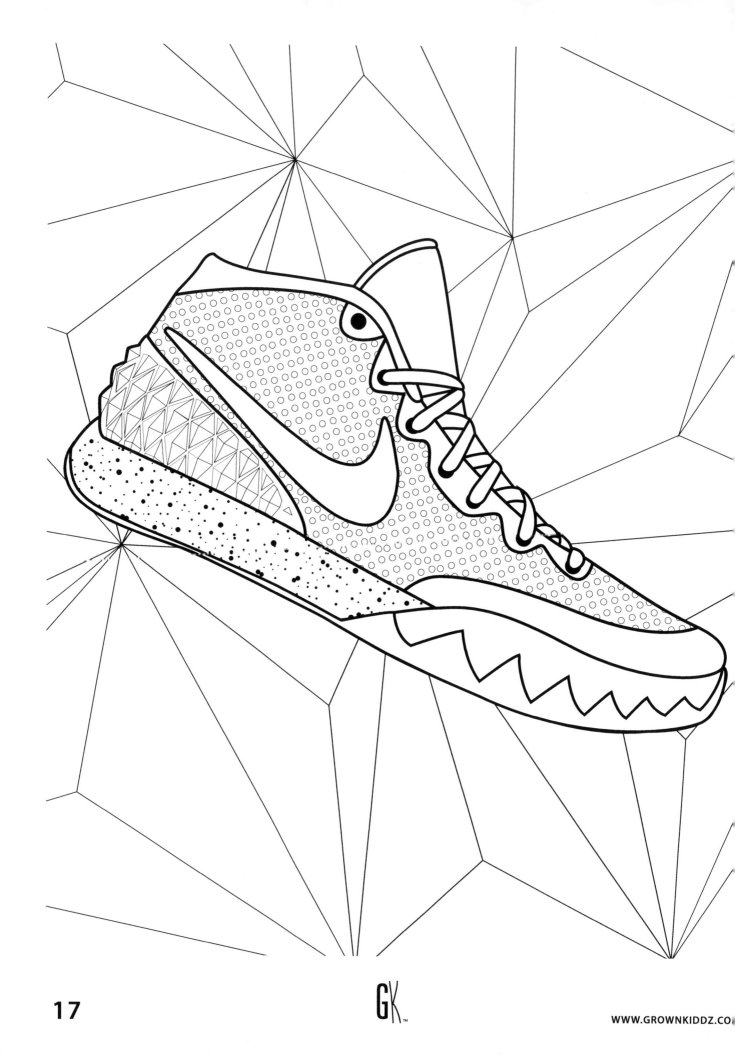

GK.

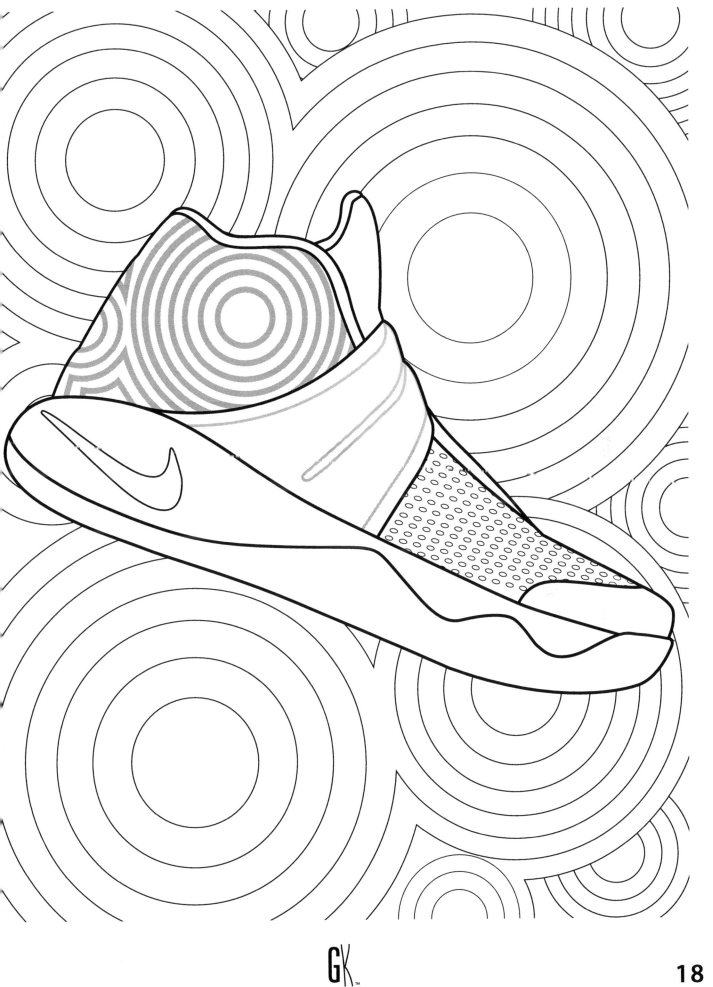

GK

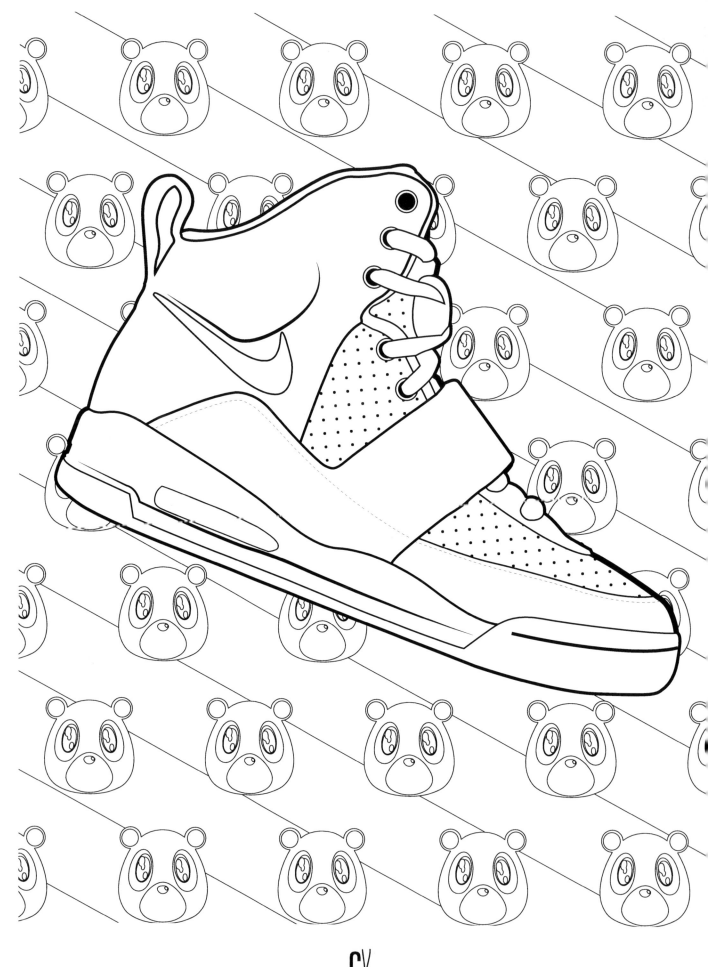

19

GK

WWW.GROWNKIDDZ.COM

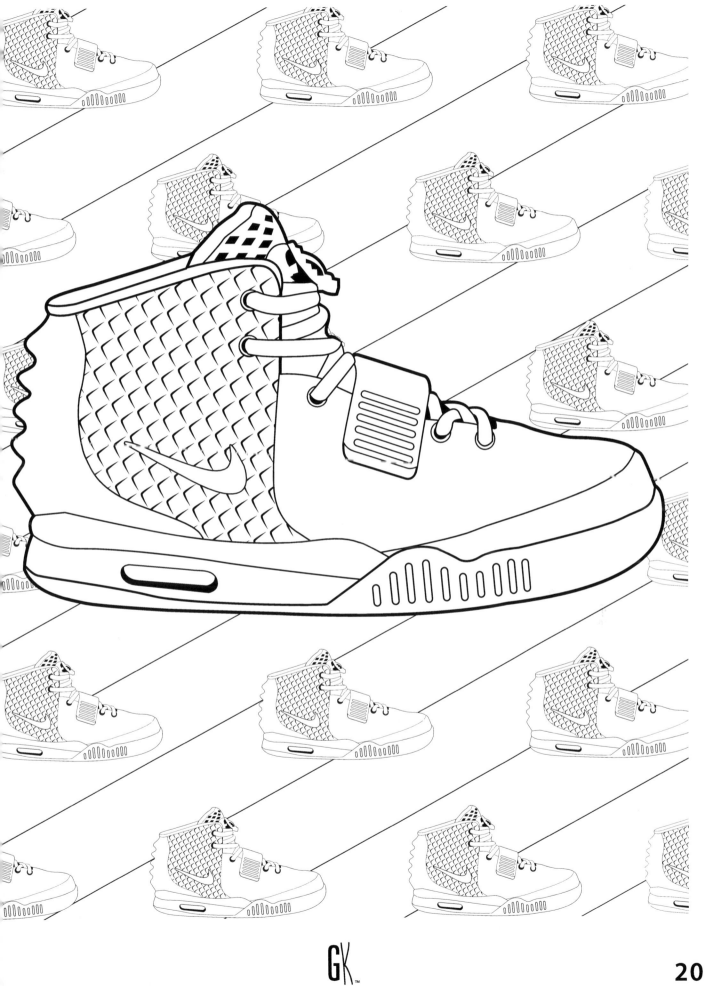

GK™

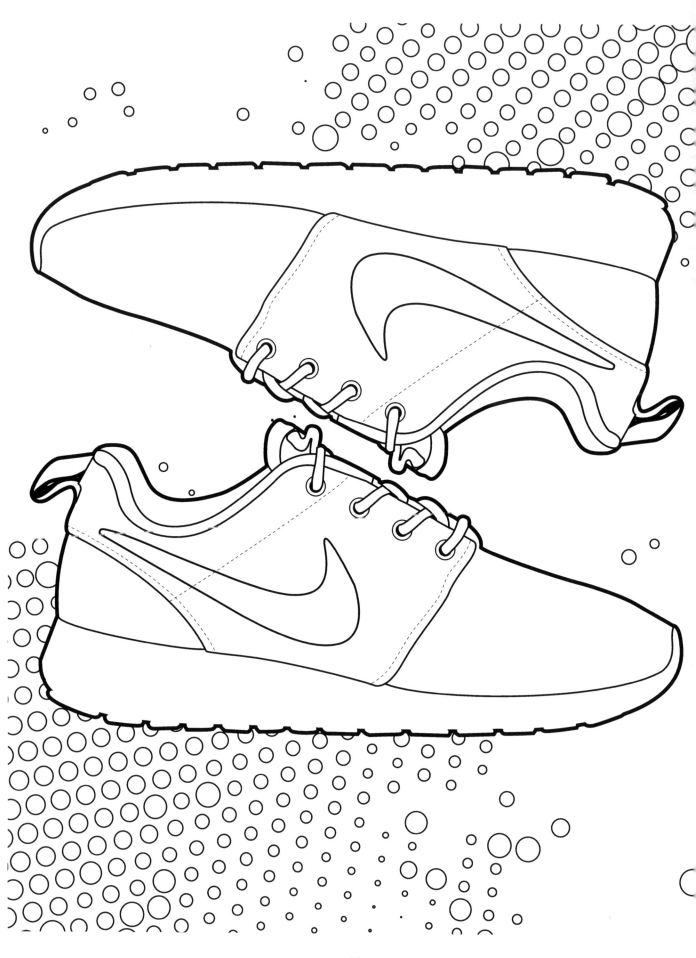

GK™

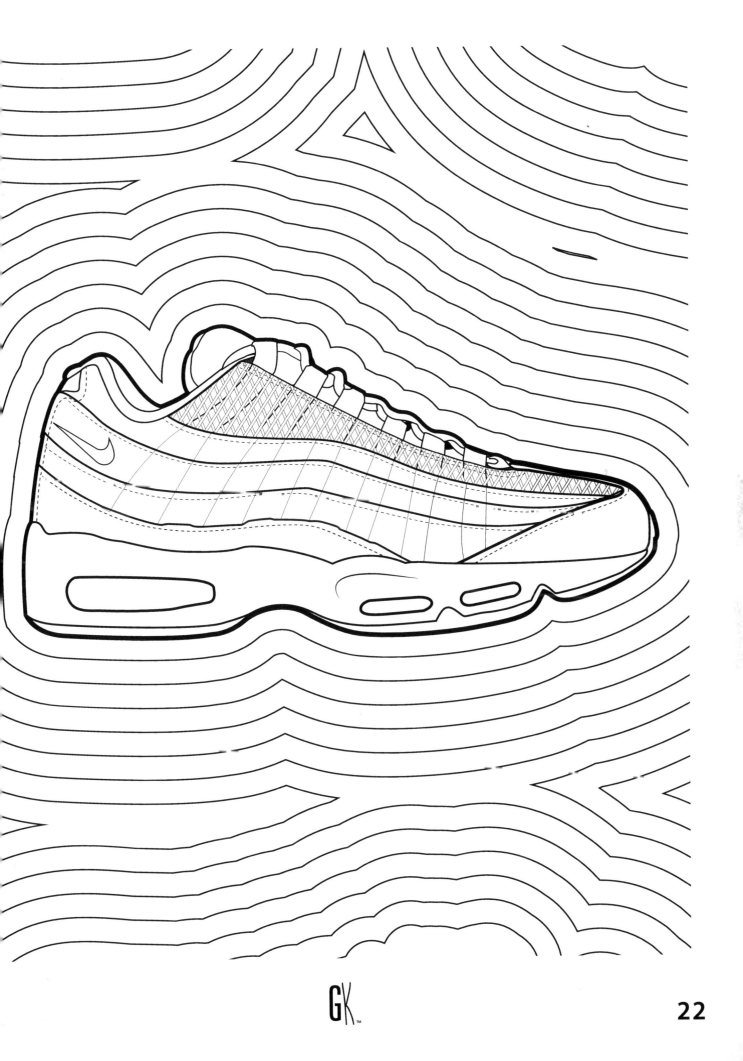

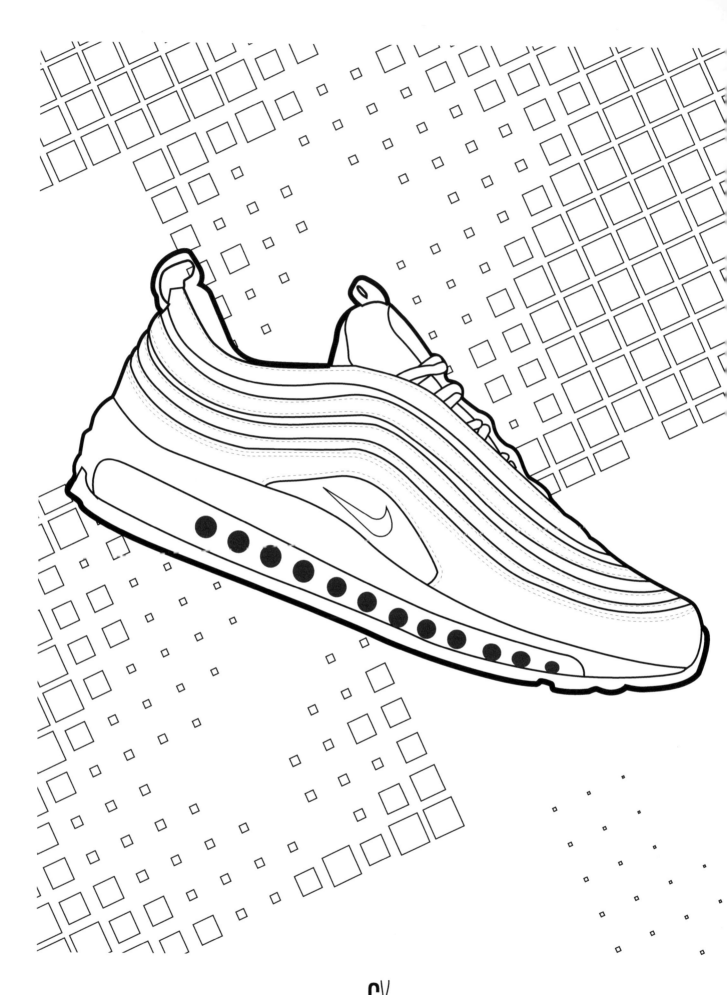

23

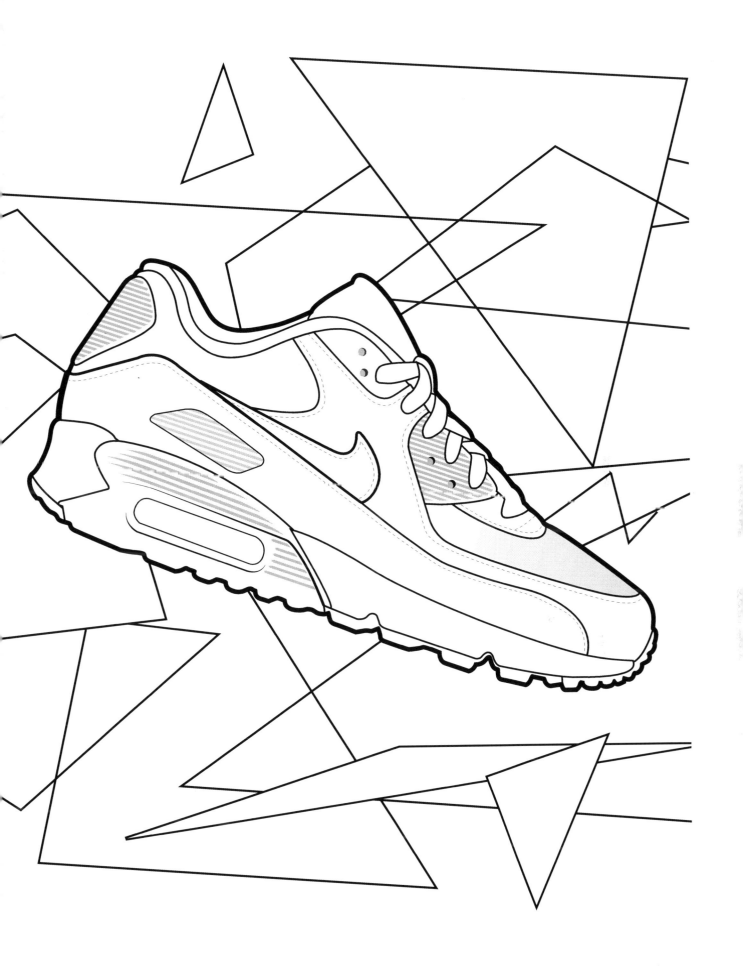

GK.

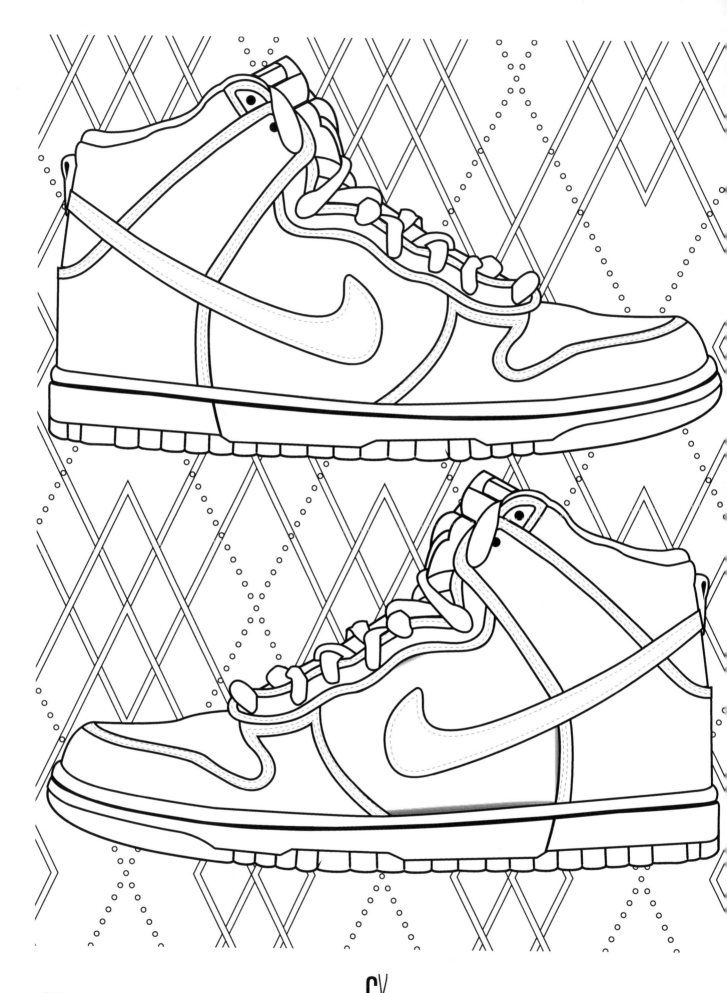

GK

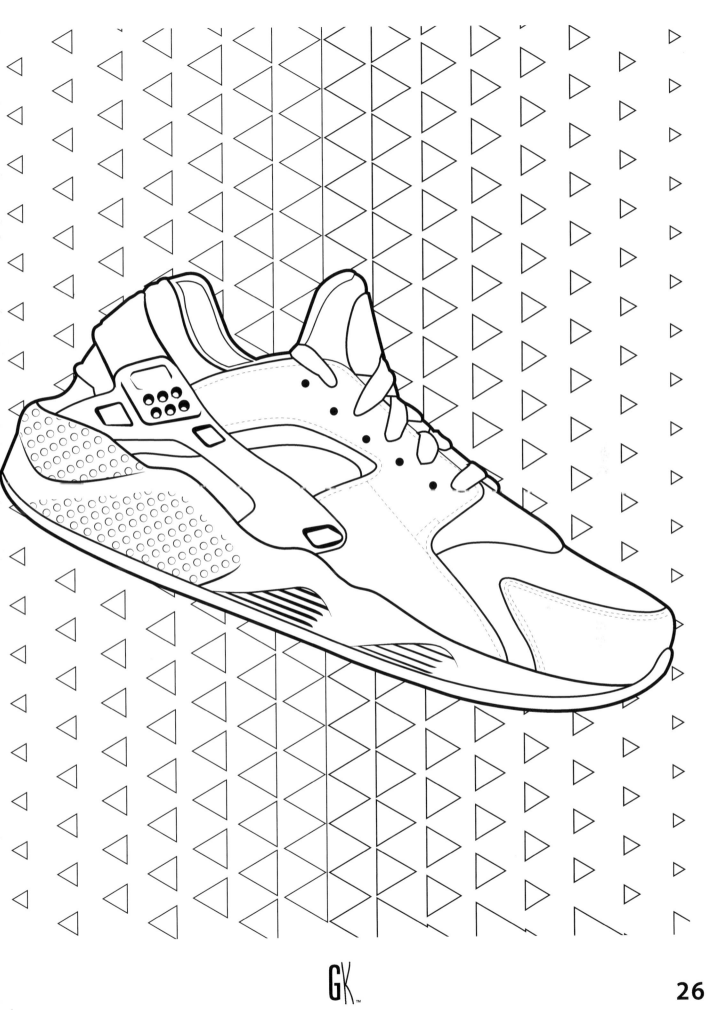

GK

Made in the USA
Middletown, DE
21 November 2020

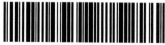